AF487928

Jenny Lin
Goes on Safari

Yutong Wu & Sean Doyle

What's that?
Dad
Reindeer

nà shì shén me?
那是什么？

Mom

xùn lù
驯鹿

What's that?
Dad
Cheetah

nà shì shén me?
那是什么？
Mom
liè bào
猎豹

What's that?
Dad
Antelope

nà shì shén me?
那是什么？
Mom
líng yáng
羚羊

What's that?
Dad
Lion

nà shì shén me?
那是什么？
Mom
shī zi
狮子

What's that?
Dad
Elephant

nà shì shén me?
那是什么？
CAS 976
Mom
dà xiàng
大象

What's that?
Dad
Zebra

nà shì shén me?
那是什么？
Mom
bān mǎ
斑马

What's that?
Dad
Giraffe

nà shì shén me?
那是什么？
Mom
cháng jǐng lù
长颈鹿

What's that?
Dad
Rhino

nà shì shén me?
那是什么？
Mom
xī niú
犀牛

Dad
Ostrich
What's that?

nà shì shén me?
那是什么？
Mom
tuó niǎo
鸵鸟

Dad Monkey
Wha

nà shì shén me?
那是什么？
that?
Mom
hóu zi
猴子

What's that?
Dad
Bison

nà shì shén me?
那是什么？
Mom
yě niú
野牛

What's that?
Dad
Camel

nà shì shén me?
那是什么？
Mom
luò tuó
骆驼

What's that?
nà shì shén me?
那是什么？
Dad
Meerkat

Mom
hú méng
狐獴

EXIT
CAS 976